Chipmunks Do What Chipmunks Do

by Julie Verne

illustrated by Laurel Aiello

Orlando   Boston   Dallas   Chicago   San Diego

Visit *The Learning Site!*

www.harcourtschool.com

What do chipmunks do in the fall?

Chipmunks know when it is fall.

Chipmunks spend time
sniffing the air.
It smells like fall.

Birds fly south for the winter.
Chipmunks stay in the woods.

They start to find food.

After the chipmunks have picked up their food, they hide it.

The food will be good to eat in the long winter.

Winter comes.
The animals in the woods
are ready.

Chipmunks are ready, too.

Like some other animals, they sleep most of the winter.

They do not sleep in a
cave or in a pond.

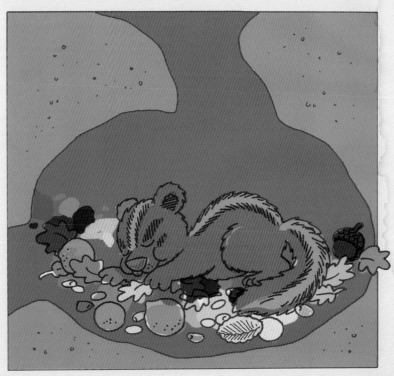

Chipmunks sleep in a
nest underground.

They may wake up and
eat the food they picked.

Most of the time, they sleep in their warm nest.

Chipmunks are smart.
They know just what to
do in the fall.